Christian Mysteries

sacred symbols

Christian Mysteries

Thames and Hudson

SYMBOL AND SACRAMENT

O ver the centuries Christians have looked on physical phenomena as symbolizing and revealing spiritual truths. Jesus himself inspired this way of looking at the world. At the beginning of his ministry he was baptised in the river Jordan – water symbolizing spiritual cleansing. As Jesus broke bread at the Last Supper, just before his crucifixion, he said that it represented his body; as he poured out wine, he declared it represented his blood.

Fearful of persecution, the early Christians used symbolism to conceal their worship of Jesus as the son of God. Jesus was often depicted as a

Frontispiece Coloured enamel panel set in jewelled frame, 13th century, showing Christ as ruler or judge, St. Mark's, Venice.

Opposite A Spanish carved gravestone with the image of a fish over a bowl, 13th century.

fish,
since the
letters of the Greek
word for fish (*ichthus*)
were seen as an acrostic
for the first letters of 'Jesus
Christ, Son of God, the
Saviour'. Christian saints were
likewise identified symbolically
in the early church. The
Revelation of St. John the Divine
refers enigmatically to a lion, a
calf, a beast with the face of a
man, and a flying eagle
worshipping before God's
throne. Fourth-century
Christians saw these
as representing,
respectively: St.
Mark,

Above Early Christian
stone with images of
concealed worship,
including a cross
disguised as an anchor
and the Greek word
for fish, *ichthus*.

Opposite *Christ in
Glory*, 12th century,
illuminated
manuscript from
Westminster Psalter,
framed by symbolic
representations of the
Four Gospels: St.
Matthew (human); St.
John (eagle); St. Luke
(bull); St. Mark (lion).

who begins his Gospel in the wilderness, the haunt of lions; St. Luke, who begins with a sacrifice, hence the bull calf; St. Matthew, who begins with the human ancestors of Jesus; and, therefore, the eagle must be St. John. The very sacraments of Christianity are effectively outward and visible signs of inward and spiritual grace. Two were instituted by Jesus (baptism and the Holy Communion) and many Christians recognize five others: confirmation, penance, holy orders, extreme unction and marriage. Legend has added its own icons and emblems to create one of the world's great bodies of belief.

Altarpiece showing the Seven Sacraments, Rogier van der Weyden, c. 1453–55.

Christic on the Tree of Life, Pacino da Bonaguido, painting, early 14th century. Divine history is symbolically arranged in a series of twelve segments.

THE CHRISTIAN YEAR

Scarcely any date in the traditional Christian year is supported by the Bible. Only the date of Jesus's crucifixion has Scriptural warranty, since it coincided with the Jewish Passover.

Yet to divide the year into a series of Christian festivals makes symbolic sense, to enable believers to rejoice in and worship different aspects of the Christian life.

Once Christ's birthday was fixed, his conception was simple to work out. Eventually other annual feasts were added to the Christian year, in particular the feasts of All Saints and All Souls, as well as the season of Lent, commemorating the forty days which Jesus spent fasting in the wilderness. Catholics celebrate on 15 August the Assumption of the mother of Jesus.

lady day

according to the Gospel of St. Luke, *the Angel Gabriel appeared on God's behalf to a virgin named Mary in the Galilean town of Nazareth and told her that God was with her and she was highly favoured. He then announced, 'You will conceive in your womb and bear a son, and you shall call his name Jesus.'*

In representing this scene artists frequently depict a white lily, symbol of Mary's purity, and the Christian church celebrates the Annunciation on 25 March, which is known as Lady Day.

omnie labia me
a apñes. tos meum
annunciabit laudem tuam.

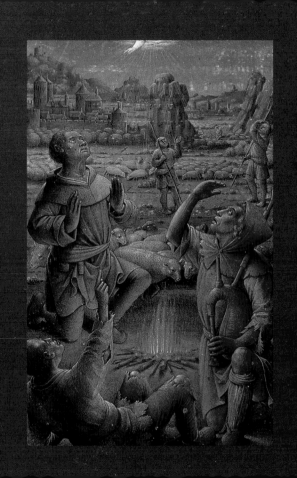

christmas

nothing in the Bible indicates the day on which Jesus was born, but three centuries or so after his birth Christians began to associate the date with the winter solstice, the day on which the sun is reborn. Hence the feast of the Nativity began to be celebrated on 25 December. The New Testament story records that Mary and her husband had arrived at Bethlehem when she was about to give birth and, according to St. Luke, they could find no room in any inn and had to stay in a stable. There Jesus was born. Finding no room in the inn, Jesus is identified with the world's outcasts. And Bethlehem, the city of King David, associates him with Israel's greatest king.

Once in Royal
David's city
   Stood a lowly
cattle shed,
   Where a Mother
laid her Baby
   In a manger
for his bed:
   Mary was that
Mother mild,
   Jesus Christ her
little Child.
   (Mrs C. F.
Alexander, 1823–95)

epiphany

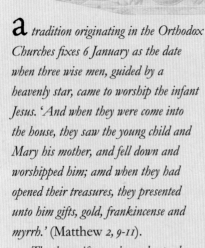

a tradition originating in the Orthodox Churches fixes 6 January as the date when three wise men, guided by a heavenly star, came to worship the infant Jesus. 'And when they were come into the house, they saw the young child and Mary his mother, and fell down and worshipped him; amd when they had opened their treasures, they presented unto him gifts, gold, frankincense and myrrh.' (Matthew 2, 9-11).

The three gifts can be understood symbolically: gold, symbol of kingship, frankincense of divinity, and myrrh (used in embalming) of Jesus's death.

Opposite The Adoration of the Kings, illumination, Jan Gossaert (called Mabuse), c. 1470– c. 1532.

Above Christ treading the Beasts between Angels, ivory cover of the Lorsch Gospels, early 9th century.

What can I give Him,
Poor as I am?
If I were a shepherd
I would bring a lamb,
If I were a Wise Man
I would do my part
Yet what I can I give Him,
Give my heart.
(*Christina Rossetti, 1830-94*)

The Temptation of Christ, painting, Duccio, 1255/60–1315/18.

lent

derived from the Old English word for spring
(lenten), *Lent comprises the forty days
before Easter (not counting Sundays).
It commemorates the forty days which Jesus
spent fasting in the wilderness, and as a result is a
time for abstinence for Christian believers.
During his time in the wilderness, Jesus resisted
temptation by the devil to misuse his supernatural
powers. These temptations were: first to turn
stones into bread; secondly to leap from a
pinnacle of the Temple, knowing that God
would save him; and thirdly to worship the devil,
who in return promised to give him authority
over all the kingdoms of the world.
Jesus's response was, 'Get thee
behind me, Satan.'*

Detail of woodcut of the Devil, from
Father Guaccius' *Coppeldium Maleficum*, 1626.

The Resurrection, detail
from the Isenheim
altarpiece, Mathias
Grünewald, *c.* 1515.

easter

On a Friday Jesus was crucified outside
Jerusalem. Three days later women came
to his tomb to anoint his body with spices,
only to find the tomb empty.

Jesus then appeared, alive, first to
the women and then to the disciples:
'But Mary stood without at the sepulchre,
weeping: and she turned herself back, and
saw Jesus standing, and knew not that it
was Jesus. Jesus saith unto her, Woman,
why weepest thou? whom seekest thou?
She, supposing him to be the gardener,
saith unto him, Sir, if thou have born
him hence, tell me where thou hast laid
him, and I will take him away.' As the
gardener, Jesus is seen to recreate the
garden of Eden fron which humanity
had been expelled.

Woodcut of *Noli me
Tangere*, Albrecht Dürer,
1471–1528. St. Mary
Magdalene mistakes
the risen Christ for a
gardener, as she weeps
by the empty tomb.

ascension

for forty days after his Resurrection Jesus stayed with his followers. Then he left them and ascended into heaven. There are various accounts of how this happened: he lifted up his hands and blessed his followers, and was carried up into heaven; he was lifted up and a cloud received him from their sight; he was taken up into heaven and sat down at the right hand of God.

Sometimes Jesus is shown with his hands outstretched in blessing. And a favourite device of many early artists was to depict God's hand, appearing from the heavens, to help pull Jesus up.

See! he lifts his hands above: Alleluya!
See! he shows the prints of love: Alleluya!
Hark! His gracious lips bestow: Alleluya!
Blessings on his Church below: Alleluya!
(*Charles Wesley, 1707-88*)

Above Passional of Christ and Antichrist, Lucas Cranach the Elder, 1521.

Opposite The Ascension, Carolingian illumination, *c.* 842.

ONGE

NA
UNI
NITŪ
UM RE
TOREM NOSTRUM ADCAE
LOS ASCEA DISSECREDI
MUS IPSI QUOQ MENTEIN
CAELESTIBUSHABITAMDE
PEREUNDEDM NOSTR

pentecost

Sometimes known as Whitsunday, the feast of
Pentecost celebrates the gift of the Holy Spirit to
the followers of Jesus and takes place fifty
days after Easter.

The Acts of the Apostles *describes
what happened. Jesus's twelve disciples were all
together in one place. 'Suddenly a sound came
from heaven like the rush of a mighty wind,
and it filled all the house where they were
sitting. And there appeared to them tongues
as of fire, distributed and resting on each one
of them.'*

*Christian art traditionally depicts the Virgin
Mary at the centre of this group, and often adds to
the symbol of fire that of the dove (the Old Testament
symbol of peace) to represent God's Holy Spirit
descending on Jesus when he was baptised.*

Mysteries of the Rosary, painting, Vincenzo Campi, 16th century. The Holy Spirit is represented as a dove.

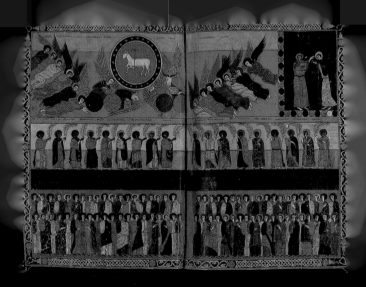

The Adoration of the Mystic Lamb, illuminated manuscript of Beatus' *Commentary on the Apocalypse,* 1047.

For all the Saints who from their labours rest,
Who thee by faith before the world confest,
Thy name, O Jesu, be for ever blest. Alleluya!
Thou wast their Rock, their Fortress and their Might;
Thou, Lord, their Captain in the well-fought fight,
Thou in the darkness drear their one true Light. Allelu

all saints

Celebrated in Western Christendom on
1 November (and by Eastern Orthodox
Christians on the first Sunday after Pentecost),
this feast commemorates all the saints and
martyrs of the Christian church. Instituted in 835,
it is known in Old English as All-Hallows, hence the name

Palm leaf and olive
branch, symbols
of triumph and peace,
respectively, from an
embossing in the early
Christian catacombs.

Hallowe'en for the previous day, which in past
times was often celebrated with
merriment and bonfires.
The saints and martyrs are usually
shown in works of art ranged in order and
worshipping Jesus, represented as the Lamb of God.

all souls

On 2 November 998, Odilo, abbot of the monastery of Cluny in France, instructed his monks to make special prayers on behalf of the dead. The practice spread through western Christendom, and 2 November became known as All Souls' Day.

Christian iconography, in sculpture and painting, often depicts the souls of the righteous being carried to heaven by angels. And an exquisite late twelfth-century or early thirteenth-century sculpture in the abbey of St. Denis, Paris, also depicts righteous souls safe in the bosom of Abraham: 'The souls of the righteous are in the hand of God; there shall no torment touch them.'

Here they live in endless life;
Transience has passed away;
Here they bloom, here thrive, they flourish,
For decayed is all decay.
(*St. Peter Damien, 1007-72*)

Above Detail from *St. Michael Raising Souls*, The Shaftesbury Psalter, mid 12th century.

Opposite *Commendation of the Souls*, Hasting Hours, *c.* 1483.

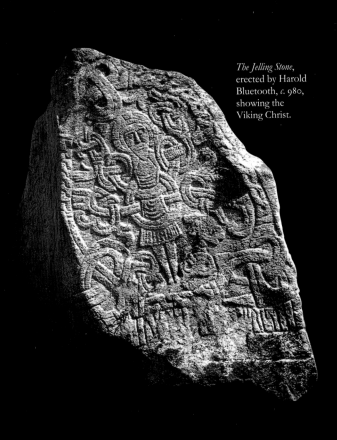

The Jelling Stone, erected by Harold Bluetooth, *c.* 980, showing the Viking Christ.

CROSS AND CRUCIFIX

to be crucified was the most humiliating death the Romans could impose. Roman citizens condemned to death (such as St. Paul) would assert their right to die by the sword, not on a cross. Yet the Cross became the most potent symbol of the glory of Christianity. Christians took up the notion that Jesus willingly submitted to crucifixion rather than call upon God, his Heavenly Father, to bring divine retribution on those who were tormenting him. He forgave those who crucified him with the words, 'Father, forgive them; they know not what they do.'

Gravestone asking for prayer for Thuathal the Wright, 9th–10th century.

Crucified for me, dear Jesus, fasten my whole self to you with the nails of your love.
(St. Bernardino of Siena, 1380-1444)

the tree of life

At one point the New Testament describes Jesus as being hanged not on a cross but on a tree. This is a reference to the story in the Book of Genesis of how Adam and Eve brought sin and death into the world by eating the forbidden fruit of a tree in the Garden of Eden. So, they were expelled from Paradise. By submitting to crucifixion, yet forgiving those who crucified him, and by rising from the dead and bringing the hope of resurrection, Jesus was seen as reversing the condemnation of Adam and Eve. The Cross on which he died thus became the tree of life.

Right Wooden plague cross, 14th century.

Opposite Tree of Death and Life, illumination, Berthold Furtmeyer, 1481.

The tree on which were fixed His dying limbs was still the chair of the Master teaching. (St. Augustine, 354-430)

the lamb of god

When John the Baptist first saw Jesus he cried, *'Behold the Lamb of God who takes away the sin of the world!'* John was referring to a lamb as a sacrificial victim. Artists have subsequently depicted Jesus as a lamb who also carries or stands by a cross (or sometimes with a banner painted with a red cross). The theme was taken up by St. John the Divine in the Book of Revelation: *'I beheld, and lo, a great multitude, which no man could number, of all nations, and kindreds, and people, and tongues, stood before the throne, and before the Lamb, clothed with white robes, and palms in their hands; and cried with a loud voice, saying, "Salvation to our God, which sitteth upon the throne, and unto the Lamb."'*

Opposite Detail, illuminated manuscript of Beatus' *Commentary*, 1047.

Above Sandstone relief of John the Baptist baptizing two noblemen, 1040.

the tortured christ

Below A medieval relief of Christ being nailed to the cross, from Dom St. Marien, Havelberg, Germany.

Opposite Altarpiece of *The Crucifixion*, Mathias Grünewald, *c.*1515.

One interpretation of Jesus's crucifixion is to see it as representing his solidarity with all those who suffer or are unjustly tortured. In the early sixteenth century Mathias Grünewald painted a superb representation of this for the Antonites of Isenheim in Alsace, monastic followers of the early Christian St. Antony of Egypt. He depicted the crucified Jesus as pock-marked and rotting, his blood-spattered body green and corrupt. The Antonites ran a hospital to nurse sufferers from disease and Grünewald's dying Jesus is symbolically identified with them.

His dying crimson like a robe
Spreads o'er his body on the Tree;
Then I am dead to all the globe,
And all the globe is dead to me.
(*Isaac Watts, 1674-1748*)

the glory of the cross

St. Paul wrote that the crucifixion seems folly to those who are perishing, but to those who are being saved it is the power of God.

The Cross was no tragedy or error on the part of Jesus but a death deliberately chosen by him in obedience to his Heavenly Father. Christian art often symbolizes this divine scheme by depicting the crucified Jesus as supported by God the Father, while the Holy Spirit in the form of a dove descends on the crucified's head. Because of this, Jesus is sometimes portrayed on the Cross as splendidly crowned and robed.

He gave power unto the sharp thorns to enter and most cruelly wound His divine and trembling head; He himself gave power to the hard nails to enter His tender feet and hands.
(*Angela of Foligno,* The Book of Divine Consolation, *c.1248-1309*)

Above Relief depicting Christ between two angels, Church of Danta Maria de Quintanilla de las Vinas, Burgos, 7th century.

Opposite The Holy Trinity, painting, Austrian School, 15th century.

instruments of the passion

'Passion', deriving from the Latin word for suffering, refers to the last week of Jesus's earthly life, above all to his trial, torture and crucifixion. Nails pierced his hands and feet as he was fixed to the cross. A crown of thorns was forced on to his head. A whip recalls his scourging. When he cried, 'I thirst,' a sponge with vinegar was applied to his lips. Alongside the hammer which drove in the nails a pair of pincers appears, which pulled out the nails at his deposition. Sometimes, too, artists depicting these instruments of the Passion include the ladder down which his dead body was dragged.

Opposite Detail from *The Agony in the Garden*, painting, Andrea Mantegna, mid 15th century.

Above Mexican stone cross carved with the face of Christ, the crown of thorns and the instruments of the Passion, 17th century.

stigmata

On the Cross, Jesus was wounded five times. Nails pierced his hands and feet. And to make sure that he was dead, a Roman soldier plunged a sword into his side. From the Greek word stigma *(sign)*, these wounds came to be called Jesus's stigmata. And throughout the Christian centuries men and women intensely meditating on the crucifixion have found such marks on their own bodies. The first person to bear these stigmata was St. Francis of Assisi, the purple wounds appearing on his body as he prayed at La Verna in 1224.

Left Biblical crown of thorns, from an Old English engraving.

Opposite The *Stigmatization of St. Francis*, wooden panel, Sassetta, 1392–1450.

the keys of st. peter

'*Who do you say that I am?' Jesus asked his disciples. Peter answered, 'The Christ, the son of the living God.' Jesus replied, 'I will give you the keys of the kingdom of heaven, and whatever you bind on earth shall be bound in heaven, and whatever you loose on earth shall be loosed in heaven.'*

St. Peter's symbol is thus a pair of keys. But he also once betrayed Jesus, claiming when Jesus was on trial never to have known him. When Peter reached Rome, he too was martyred, but (legend has it) insisted that he should be crucified upside down, so as to be lower than his Lord – a second symbol of this disciple is a cross turned upside-down.

Opposite **Death of St. Peter**, painting, Giotto (1266–1336).

Below Stone statue of St. Peter with the keys of the Kingdom of Heaven, 12th century.

the cross of st. andrew

Below Stone saltire cross, 7th century.

Opposite St Andrew on his saltire cross, illumination from the Book of Hours of John the Fearless, Duke of Burgundy, 1406–15.

a *fisherman, St. Andrew was recruited, with his brother Simon, to be the first disciple of Jesus. A fourth-century tradition tells that he was crucified, but remained alive for two days, preaching the Gospel from the cross. A yet later tradition declares that the cross was in the form of an X (the saltire cross), representing the first letter of the Greek word for Christ.*

Andrew is the patron saint of Greece, Russia and Scotland, whose national flag is a saltire cross.

Jesus said, Follow me: and I will make you fishers of men. (Matthew 4, 19)

QUEEN OF HEAVEN

madonna is Italian for 'My Lady' and signifies the mother of Jesus, the Blessed Virgin Mary, particularly when in art she is depicted carrying her son Jesus, either in her womb or on her knee.

The New Testament asserts that she conceived Jesus without losing her virginity. And since she was the mother of one who brought grace and forgiveness to the world, eventually many Christians have looked to her as their greatest protectress among all the saints.

In spite of her exalted state, Mary is also a symbol of Christian humility. Nevertheless her depiction often reflects her glory, as she is seen with a halo of stars and on a crescent moon.

Mother and maiden
Was never none but she;
Well may such a lady
Goddes mother be.
(Fifteenth-century poem, anon.)

Opposite Detail of *The Immaculate Conception*, painting, Diego Velazquez, 1599–1660.

'ave maria'

according to the Gospel of St. Luke, the Angel Gabriel declared to the mother of Jesus, 'Hail Mary, full of grace; the Lord is with thee… blessed is the fruit of thy womb.' Since the Middle Ages, this has been one of Christendom's most celebrated prayers: 'Ave Maria, gratia plena; Dominus tecum; benedicta tu in mulieribus; et benedictus fructus ventris tui, Jesus.' To this many add the request, 'Holy Mary, mother of God, pray for us sinners now and at the hour of our death.' Many Christians use this prayer in connection with the rosary, a string of beads. While telling the beads of the rosary, the faithful repeatedly pray, 'Ave Maria'.

Opposite Madonna of the Rosary, painting, Caravaggio, *c.* 1600.

christ-child

images of the Infant Jesus have offered scope for rich symbolism. Usually he is guarded by his mother, who may well be crowned Queen of Heaven and carry a sceptre as well as her divine son. The child is often portrayed seated upright, blessing the world. Other artists include the Virgin Mary's mother, St. Anna.

Leonardo da Vinci's The Virgin of the Rocks *draws* on another rich symbolic tradition. Here Jesus's mother is blessing her son while with her other hand caressing the infant John the Baptist (identified by one of his symbols, a cross with a long stem), whose mother was Mary's cousin. In Leonardo's painting John is kneeling in prayer, while Jesus blesses him. And an angel behind the Christ-child holds the chubby divine baby upright.

Opposite The Virgin of the Rocks, painting, Leonardo da Vinci, *c.* 1483.

pietà

Pietà, *Italian for 'pity', in art refers to depictions of the Blessed Virgin Mary holding the body of her dead son across her knees. Among the most exquisite is Michelangelo's in St. Peter's, Rome; among the most sombre, one by Rembrandt.*

Michelangelo's Pietà *was criticized because he made the mother of Jesus seem younger than her son. His reply was that because of her purity she possessed eternal youth. He also clad her in brilliantly sculpted clothing which (in John Ruskin's words) represented the spirit of repose, 'repose saintly and severe'. Ruskin added that the undulation of the clothing follows the dances of angels.*

the assumption

although the notion that after her death the Blessed Virgin Mary was taken up body and soul into heaven was declared an official belief of Roman Catholics only in 1950, her Assumption has long been relished as a subject of Christian art. In the fifteenth and sixteenth centuries a galaxy of artists depicted the scene, in particular Girolamo da Vicenza, Titian and the limewood sculptor Tilman Riemenschneider, transforming the event into one of immense glamour.

protectress

One of the most powerful symbols of the Madonna is her role as protectress of humanity. Usually she is represented in a cloak, which she opens wide to shelter vulnerable men and women who share her humanity and desire her care.

They are often depicted as the most powerful in the world — sovereigns, Popes, bishops, noble lords and ladies — as well as the humble folk who also display some part of Mary's own humility.

But God has chosen the foolish things of the world to confound the wise; and God hath chosen the weak things of the world to confound the things which are mighty. (I Corinthians *1, 27*)

Opposite The Blessed Virgin Mary, painted central panel of a polyptych, Piero della Francesca, 1445.

Below Madonna carrying in her womb God the Father and his Crucified Son, painted wood, 15th century.

Black Madonna, painted
wood, Church of Santa
Maria Liberatrice, Ancona,
16th century.

black madonna

Over the
centuries the smoke of candles has
transformed statues of the Madonna into
Black Virgins. Some of them have become famous:
at Rocamadour in France; at Czestochowa in Poland; at
Altötting in Bavaria. All are centres of pilgrimage. Why are
these statues never cleaned? Because of the Christian habit of
assuming that the Jewish scriptures (the Old Testament) refer
to the Christian faith. In the Song of Solomon a woman
reciting a love-poem sings, 'I am black but comely.'
Christians took this to be a prophecy about
the Blessed Virgin Mary. So, it
was supposed, any black statue
of the Virgin could be a
perfect representation
of the true
Madonna.

LEGEND

though often historically dubious, legends can evoke potent echoes in the human psyche.

The Christian tradition is replete with them, many surrounded with expressive symbols. Christians, for example, asked what happened to the cup from which Jesus and his disciples drank at their last meal on earth, and without any real grounds for their claims many places in Christendom claim to have inherited it. Others wondered what had happened to the shroud in which Jesus was wrapped at his burial.

Such legendary symbols have been matched in the Christian tradition by remarkable images, many derived from the imagination of the Christian fathers.

Opposite Souls Cross Over the Narrow Bridge, fresco, 13th century.

Pure
religion and
undefiled before God
and the Father is this,
to visit the fatherless
and widows in their
affliction, and to
keep himself
unspotted from
the world.
(*St. James the Great*)

the pilgrim

St. James the Great is the patron saint
of pilgrims. Although he was executed and
buried in the Holy Land, his body is said
to rest today at Santiago de Compostela
in Spain, which (after Jerusalem and Rome)
is the most important pilgrimage centre in
Christendom. Christian art depicts him covered in
symbols: a cockleshell, from the shores of
Galicia; a pilgrim's staff; a hat, since pilgrims
travel through inhospitable lands during
the heat of the day; and a flask for drink.
And whereas most saints are depicted
barefoot, St. James, because of his long journeys,
often wears boots.

Opposite left *St. James of Compostela*, sculpture, 12th century, bearing a
staff and a purse decorated with a cockleshell.

Opposite right Cross with logos symbol from the Episcopal throne
at Torcello Cathedral, early medieval.

holy blood, holy grail

The legend of the Holy Grail records that the chalice which Jesus used at his Last Supper with his disciples was retrieved by a devout Jew, Joseph of Arimathea, who gave a tomb to Jesus. As Jesus hung on the cross, Joseph, it is said, used this chalice to catch some of his spilled blood.

The story becomes yet more fanciful. Joseph, it was claimed, next visited England. Arriving at Glastonbury, he left the Grail there, where it was buried and long forgotten. Certainly there is no trace at Glastonbury of such a symbol today; but many other places still claim to possess a drop of Jesus's Holy Blood.

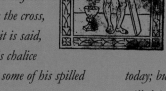

Woodcut illustrating *The Imitation of Christ*, 15th century.

Angels holding the Holy Grail, illumination from the Playfair
Book of Hours, late 15th century.

the shroud of turin

Joseph of Arimathea, says St. Matthew's Gospel, took the body of the dead Jesus 'and wrapped it in a clean linen cloth.' From 1578, in the chapel of the Dukes of Savoy close by Turin cathedral, a length of ivory-coloured material bearing a strange image of a bearded man was exhibited as the same shroud. The image displays wounds in exactly the same places as those inflicted on Jesus at his crucifixion.

Today, most scholars believe that this shroud is a fake. Its history cannot be traced back beyond the fourteenth century. Yet, as the French poet Paul Claudel wrote, the image on the shroud is 'so frightening and yet so beautiful that one can escape it only by worship.'

This much, and this is all we know,
   They are supremely blest,
   Have done with sin, and care, and woe,
   And with their Saviour rest.
   (John Newton, 1725-1807)

Opposite Head of Christ, detail from the Turin shroud.

the glastonbury thorn

Below Woodcut, Honor Howard-Mercer for *St. Joseph of Arimathæa*, W.E.C. Baynes, 1929.

Opposite Joseph of Arimathea Planting His Staff at Glastonbury, illumination, Brotherhood of St. Seraphim of Sarov, 1978.

When Joseph of Arimathea came to England, he bequeathed to Glastonbury not only the Holy Grail but also his staff. Joseph stuck it into the ground, where it took root and was transformed into a hawthorn.

Glastonbury hawthorns do bloom in May and around Christmas; but whether they are descended from the staff of Joseph of Arimathea is a moot point. The monks of Glastonbury abbey certainly promoted the story, which brought them pilgrims and renown. In the mid seventeenth century the original tree was destroyed by Puritans, but it is claimed that cuttings survived.

S. JOSEPH OF ARIMATHEA

chi-rho

The monogram chi-rho derives from the first two letters of the Greek word for Christ, and is represented by the symbols X and P, Greek capital letters. One fifth-century bronze cross is fascinating for incorporating these letters with two other Greek ones, 'alpha' and 'omega', the first and last letters of the Greek alphabet and another symbol of Jesus: "'I am Alpha and Omega, the beginning and the ending," saith the Lord, "which is, and which was, and which is to come.'" (Revelation 1,8)

I know much Greek and Latin. I have still to learn the alphabet of how to become a saint. *(St. Arsenius, d. 250)*

Above Bronze cross with monogram *chi-rho* and the symbols 'alpha' and 'omega', 5th century.

Opposite Jewelry depicting *chi-rho*, 4th century.

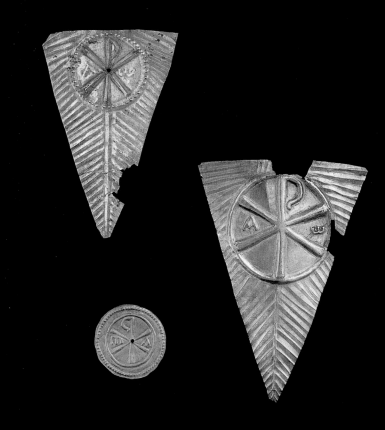

st. veronica

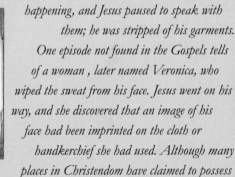

as Jesus made his way to be crucified, carrying
his own cross, the four Gospels add these details:
a man named Simon of Cyrene was forced
to help carry the cross; women lamented what was
happening, and Jesus paused to speak with
them; he was stripped of his garments.
One episode not found in the Gospels tells
of a woman , later named Veronica, who
wiped the sweat from his face. Jesus went on his
way, and she discovered that an image of his
face had been imprinted on the cloth or
handkerchief she had used. Although many
places in Christendom have claimed to possess
this cloth, the Roman clergy insisted that theirs
was the true image, vera icon, hence the name 'Veronica'.

Opposite Christ Making His Way to His Crucifixion, stone altarpiece, c. 1500.

Above Veronica with the Sudarium, painting, early 15th century.

the cosmic battle

'And there was war in heaven, Michael and his angels fought against the dragon, and the dragon fought and his angels, and prevailed not, neither was their place found any more in heaven. And the great dragon was cast out, that old serpent, called the devil and Satan, which deceiveth the whole world: he was cast out unto the earth, and his angels were cast out with him (Revelation *12, 7-9*). St. Michael is thus often portrayed winged and sometimes riding a charger, plunging his spear or sword into a serpent. A second symbol of Michael the Archangel is a pair of scales, with which he weighs the souls of the dead.

Be sober, be vigilant, for your adversary the devil, as a roaring lion, walketh about, seeking whom he may devour. (*St. Peter*)

Above The Archangel Michael Vanquishing the Devil, illumination, 1490.

Opposite The Archangel Michael and His Angels Defeating the Forces of Evil, illumination, 11th century.

DEVS QVI

revelation

the last book of the Bible, *the* Revelation of St. John the Divine, *overflows with imagery and symbol, including this compelling vision of Jesus glorified: 'I saw seven golden candlesticks, and in the midst of the seven golden candlesticks, one like unto the Son of man, clothed with a garment down to his foot, and girt about the paps with a golden girdle. His head and his hairs were white like wool, as white as snow, and his eyes were as a flame of fire, and his feet like unto fine brass, as if they burned in a furnace: and his voice as the sound of many waters. And he had in his right hand seven stars: and out of his mouth went a sharp two-edged sword: and his countenance was as the sun shineth in his strength.'*

Apocalypse of St. Sever, illumination, 11th century.

Sources of the illustrations